Oh No, Not My New

RED DRESS

SADIE R. ALSTON

ILLUSTRATED BY DR. LEE SMITH

AuthorHouse™
1663 Liberty Drive
Bloomington, IN 47403
www.authorhouse.com
Phone: 833-262-8899

Because of the dynamic nature of the Internet, any web addresses or links contained in this book may have changed since publication and may no longer be valid. The views expressed in this work are solely those of the author and do not necessarily reflect the views of the publisher, and the publisher hereby disclaims any responsibility for them.

This book is printed on acid-free paper.

ISBN: 978-1-6655-3145-0 (sc)
ISBN: 978-1-6655-3146-7 (e)

Library of Congress Control Number: 2021913888

Print information available on the last page.

Published by AuthorHouse 09/08/2021

authorHOUSE®

Dedication

After many years of teaching and reading, this book is a fulfillment of one of my most cherished dreams that God has brought to pass in my life.

I have spent many days reading to students in an elementary school setting, so for this first book, I am dedicating this book to all of my students who took their first school journey with me in Kindergarten at Lakewood Elementary School in Durham, NC. Your parents planted the seed of wanting to know in each of you. You came into my classroom of wonder, exploring, and learning and I watered you down really good and you blossomed into beautiful flowers that I will never forget. I will be forever grateful for all that we learned together. We had many laughs and many tears, and an abundance of good times, so this book is for you.

Oh No, Not My New Red Dress.

Mrs. Sadie Riggins Alston

It was close to the end of the summer, one bright, clear, sunny day. Sadie's mom had gone shopping.

When Sadie's mom came home from shopping, Sadie was outside playing by the big tree in her yard. Mom gave her a pretty blue bag.

Sadie was so excited, she ran to the porch and sat down to open her pretty blue bag. When she reached into the bag she felt something soft.

Sadie reached into the bag and pulled the soft thing out that her mother had bought her. It was a brand new pretty red dress.

Sadie was so excited that she hugged her mom and said, "Thank you mom!"

The next day was the first day of school after the summer break. Sadie decided that she would wear her new red dress to school.

When Sadie came into the kitchen her mom hugged her and said, "You look so pretty, Sadie." Sadie was so excited to go to school in her new red dress.

Sadie went outside to wait for the bus. As she waits, along comes her dog, Spot.

When Spot saw her, he became very excited.

Spot had been playing in a mud puddle that morning. When he came near Sadie she said, "No, No, Spot!"

Spot ran and jumped on Sadie. Sadie said, "Oh no! Not my new red dress!" She became sad.

Spot ran away wondering why Sadie didn't want to play with him.

Sadie's mom came outside and saw her crying. She asked, "What happened, Sadie?" Sadie said, "Spot jumped on my new red dress."

Mom said, "Oh no! Not your new red dress!

The End.

Printed in the United States
by Baker & Taylor Publisher Services